MW00581707

Christmas Carols For Guitar 2

Graded arrangements of 12 favourite Christmas songs for acoustic, fingerstyle and classical guitar

Arranged by James Akers

Copyright © 2021 GMI - Guitar & Music Institute

www.guitarandmusicinstitute.com

ISBN 978-1-7399473-2-3

First published in Scotland in 2021 by GMI - Guitar & Music Institute

All rights reserved. No part of this publication may be reproduced or distributed in any form or by any means, or stored in a data base or retrieval system, without the prior written permission of the author.

Cover - creative commons

PLEASE NOTE THAT DOWNLOAD INSTRUCTIONS FOR THE FREE PACK THAT ACCOMPANIES THIS BOOK IS FOUND ON PAGE 45.

Christmas Carols For Guitar 2

Graded arrangements of 12 favourite Christmas songs for acoustic, fingerstyle and classical guitar

Arranged by James Akers

Table Of Contents

A foreword by Ged Brockie of GMI,

This is the second book, launched in consecutive years, in what has now become the James Akers series of graded Christmas songs. In 2020, James published his first Christmas book through GMI to test the water. Both James and GMI were delighted by the response given by the guitar playing public.

Here is a small selection of shortened reviews from that first release…

1. *Really like this approach and, while I focused very happily on the advanced arrangements, it was nice to know the intermediate options were there if I wanted to 'fast track' to a complete-sounding Christmas favourite.*

2. *Brilliant idea - each Carol has three different versions - easy, intermediate and advanced, which means that whatever stage you are at you will be able to play these.*

3. *Absolutely love this book! I decided 1 year ago to take up guitar again, after nearly 40 years, and am a a point where I need more practice materials that is easy enough for me to play, yet, challenging enough to continue growing.*

4. *Brilliant idea - each Carol has three different versions - easy, intermediate and advanced, which means that whatever stage you are at you will be able to play these.*

With reviews like that, which are all visible on Amazon, it did not take much imagination for James and GMI to work hard and give people more of the same, which is exactly what you have in front of you now. Twelve new Christmas carols. Each song offered in three versions of technical difficulty from easy to expert not forgetting the bonus extra song!

The song arrangements found here are firm Christmas favourites and if you do own the first book in the series, these choices will prove a wonderful compliment to that initial volume.

There is real depth to this book and the accompanying resources found within the accompanying download. Personally, I feel that these arrangements, particularly the advanced versions, offer a real challenge and are a stunning example not only of James's undoubted performance talents, but his arranging prowess as well.

Regardless of whether it's Christmas or not, you'll find it's always a pleasure to play these wonderful songs. Christmas carols that have, in a way, metamorphosed into evergreen classics.

Ged Brockie

Introduction

This book aims to provide guitarists of all levels with practical, appealing arrangements of well-known Christmas songs in both standard notation and tab. Each song appears in three versions. The first is simply the tune itself, set in a convenient key so that the beginner guitarist, in the early stages of their progress can give a convincing, recognisable rendition of the melody. This version includes chord symbols to allow for the beginner to be accompanied by a more experienced player or teacher or practise playing the chords themselves. The second version is the same melody with an added bass-line and occasional chords to allow the suggestion of harmony and provide more of a challenge to the advancing guitarist. This version employs a tonal harmonic idiom, as might be heard in traditional choral arrangements of these songs. The third version is a fully realised chordal arrangement with more advanced harmonies, utilising the full range of the fingerboard and a variety of techniques and idioms. This allows a more musically complete performance and should be a rewarding challenge for the accomplished player.

It is intended that this book will see the beginner guitarist through several years of study, allowing them to chart their progress over successive festive seasons and perform the tunes everyone wants to hear at Christmas. It is also intended to be a useful resource for teachers, providing them with a collection of pieces to suit pupils of all levels and technical requirements.

James Akers

Deck the Halls

The Melody of Deck the Halls originally dates from the 16th century, a Welsh winter carol entitled, Nos Galan. English words were provided in the 1860s and a popular Christmas classic was the result.

The advanced version of Deck the Halls is arranged in a playful cartoon music style, using a variety of techniques and timbres, sudden changes of mood, harmony and tempo while maintaining the original melody.

Watch James perform the advanced version by pointing your mobile phone or tablet with a QR code reader at the box on the right.

Or go to the following URL:

https://www.youtube.com/watch?v=7p7vVmTIWCw

Deck the Halls: Beginners

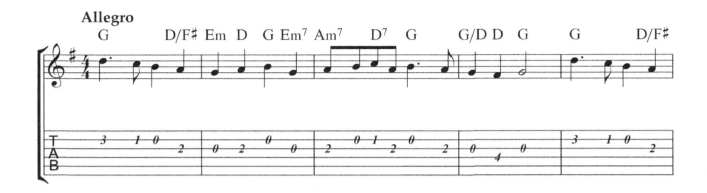

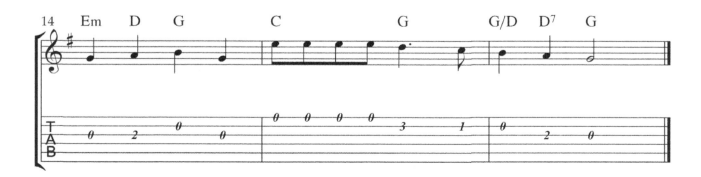

Deck the Halls: Intermediate

Deck the Halls: Advanced

Scherzando

13

Hark the Herald Angels Sing

Hark the Herald Angels Sing, is an English carol dating from the 18th century with words by Charles Wesley, the founder of Methodism. The well-known melody was adapted from a cantata by the composer Felix Mendelssohn and the two combined in 1855 to great acclaim.

The advanced arrangement of Hark the Herald Angels is in a jazz style with a staccato walking bass and swing rhythms. You could try adding some percussive effects in the rests.

Watch James perform the advanced version by pointing your mobile phone or tablet with a QR code reader at the box on the right.

Or go to the following URL:

https://www.youtube.com/watch?v=EgwGgD-55F8

Hark the Herald Angels Sing: Beginners

Hark the Herald Angels Sing: Intermediate

Hark the Herald Angels: Advanced

I Saw Three Ships

I Saw Three Ships, is a traditional carol dating from the 17th century. Its simple melody and lilting triple time rhythm have contributed to its long-term popularity.

The advanced I Saw Three Ship, was inspired by folk guitar styles and includes strumming, and modal harmonies and features the familiar melody in different octaves and keys.

Watch James perform the advanced version by pointing your mobile phone or tablet with a QR code reader at the box on the right.

Or go to the following URL:

https://www.youtube.com/watch?v=xtmdqxlp-BY

I Saw Three Ships: Beginners

Allegretto

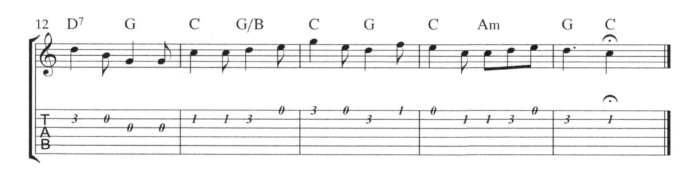

I Saw Three Ships: Intermediate

I Saw Three Ships: Advanced

In the Bleak Midwinter

In The Bleak Midwinter is a relatively modern carol, written by the great English composer Gustav Holst, famed for his Planet's Suite and settings of English folk songs.

The advanced arrangement of In the Bleak Midwinter, adds an arpeggiated accompaniment to the melody, largely keeping to Holst's original harmonies. A short introduction employing parallel fifths has been added, in traditional tonal harmony this was frowned upon but Holst often made use of this sonority in his music.

Watch James perform the advanced version by pointing your mobile phone or tablet with a QR code reader at the box on the right.

Or go to the following URL:

https://www.youtube.com/
watch?v=1sqd37p6bfU

In The Bleak Midwinter: Beginners

Rosetti   Holst

In The Bleak Midwinter: Intermediate

Rosetti

Holst

In The Bleak Midwinter: Advanced

Rosetti

Holst

Joy to the World

The melody of Joy to the World was composed by the great baroque opera and oratorio composer George Frederick Handel. It is a more ornate tune than the others, even in the beginner's version, with syncopated rhythms and quick passing notes.

The advanced Joy to the World is arranged in a baroque style, in keeping with the origins of the melody. A short overture has been added and the tune harmonised in imitation of Handel with passages in thirds and imitative counterpoint.

Watch James perform the advanced version by pointing your mobile phone or tablet with a QR code reader at the box on the right.

Or go to the following URL:

https://www.youtube.com/watch?v=DB0kn-9hRfE

Joy to the World: Beginners

Handel

Joy to the World: Intermediate

Handel

Joy to the World: Advanced

6 to D

Handel

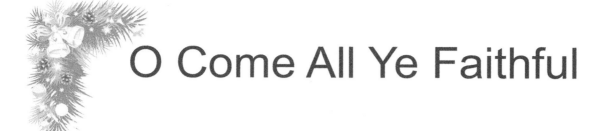

O Come All Ye Faithful

The melody of O Come All Ye Faithful has been attributed to various composers including King João IV of Portugal, resulting in it sometimes being referred to as the "Portuguese hymn."

The advanced arrangement of O Come all ye Faithful, has been rendered in the style of a Habanera, using the distinctive dotted rhythm ostinato and harmonies of the style.

Watch James perform the advanced version by pointing your mobile phone or tablet with a QR code reader at the box on the right.

Or go to the following URL:

https://www.youtube.com/watch?v=Br6uTBh9RIo

O Come All Ye Faithful: Beginners

O Come All Ye Faithful: Intermediate

O Come All Ye Faithful: Advanced

Alla Habanera

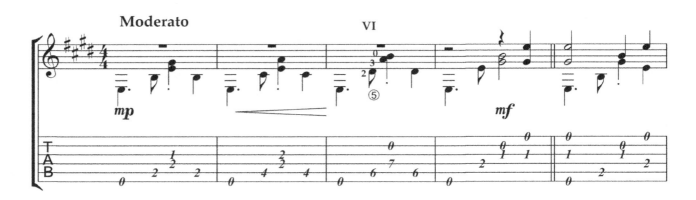

44

GET YOUR DOWNLOAD PACK WHICH SUPPORTS THIS PUBLICATION

1. Use a QR code reader and point at box below to download file.

2. OR paste this URL in a browser and then follow the download instructions:

https://gmiguitarshop.com/products/free-download-for-christmas-carols-for-guitar

3. OR go to https://gmiguitarshop.com and uses the search area at the top right of the website and search "Christmas Carols 2" and you'll see the download.

WHAT IS INCLUDED?

- Diagrams in PDF format of all chords played in each of the twelve beginner arrangements.

- mp3 files of all advanced version performances.

- Accompanying guitar tracks for all beginner arrangements.

PLEASE NOTE: The download is compressed by a utility programme named WINRAR which is commonly used by PC owners. If your PC does not see the compressed file, search "WINRAR DOWNLOAD" in your favourite browser to be directed to the main WINRAR website.

If you have a Mac computer, tablet or cell phone and encounter any difficulty opening the compressed file please use a search engine and search "opening WINRAR files on a Mac". There are many sites and Youtube videos which offer simple to execute ways on how to do this.

O Little Town Of Bethlehem

O Little Town of Bethlehem features a text by Philip Brooks, an American priest, adapted to a folk song melody, arranged, and harmonised by the English composer Vaughan Williams.

The advanced arrangement of O Little Town of Bethlehem is in a jazz style with an added introduction and a solo which uses the famous "rhythm changes" that feature in many jazz standards.

Watch James perform the advanced version by pointing your mobile phone or tablet with a QR code reader at the box on the right.

Or go to the following URL:

https://www.youtube.com/watch?v=EaEHSGM1uO8

O Little Town of Bethlehem: Beginners

O Little Town of Bethlehem: Intermediate

O Little Town of Bethlehem: Advanced

Once In Royal David's City

Once in Royal David's City was published in 1848 in a collection of Hymns for children and is, famously, the opening piece in the Festival of Nine Lessons and Carols from King's College, Cambridge when a boy treble opens proceedings by singing an unaccompanied verse of this popular melody.

The advanced setting of Once in Royal David's City begins, like the choral arrangement, with the melody played unaccompanied, using artificial harmonics. Thereafter, the accompaniment employs a range of broadly textured chords to support the affecting melody.

Watch James perform the advanced version by pointing your mobile phone or tablet with a QR code reader at the box on the right.

Or go to the following URL:

https://www.youtube.com/watch?v=6mudkXqpEUw

Once In Royal David's City: Beginners

Once In Royal David's City: Intermediate

Once In Royal David's City: Advanced

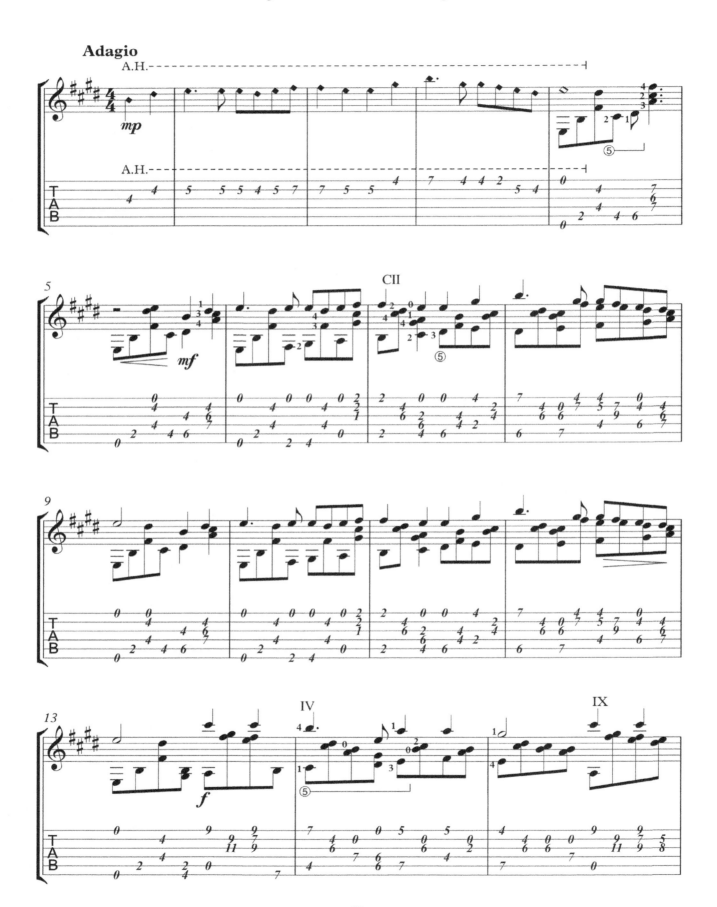

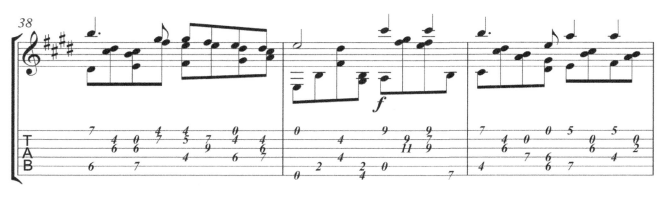

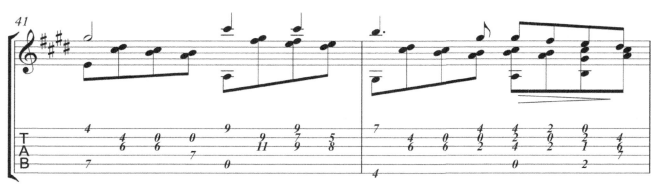

The Coventry Carol

The Coventry Carol dates from the 16th century and demonstrates some distinctive features of music of this era, in particular the Picardy (major) third within a minor key. The melancholy nature of the melody contrasts with the more cheerful tenor of the average Christmas carol but is in keeping with the subject matter of the text.

The advanced Coventry Carol is an extended Fantasia on the tune inspired by the great English lutenist composer, John Dowland. It employs Renaissance style textures and harmonies and quotations from Dowand's most famous work, the Lachrimae Pavan.

Watch James perform the advanced version by pointing your mobile phone or tablet with a QR code reader at the box on the right.

Or go to the following URL:

https://www.youtube.com/watch?v=c7QP3Uezox0

The Coventry Carol: Beginners

The Coventry Carol: Intermediate

The Coventry Carol: Advanced

Fantasia on the Coventry Carol

The First Nowell

The First Nowell, dates from the 19th century and is thought to have been of Cornish origin. The tune has a simple, repetitive structure making it easy to remember and a perennial Christmas favourite.

The advanced version of The First Nowell is in a baroque ground bass style, adapted from Henry Purcell's Evening Hymn. The suggested fingerings in the variation section employ the popular campanella technique beloved of baroque lutenists-and modern classical guitarists when performing baroque music.

Watch James perform the advanced version by pointing your mobile phone or tablet with a QR code reader at the box on the right.

Or go to the following URL:

https://www.youtube.com/watch?v=2QdrXbkDb7w

The First Nowell: Beginners

The First Nowell: Intermediate

Andante

The First Nowell: Advanced

The Holly and the Ivy

The text of The Holly and the Ivy suggests it has its origins in the medieval period, however, the melody associated with it today was only written down for the first time in 1911 by the famous musicologist Cecil Sharp.

The Holly and the Ivy advanced is arranged in a contemporary folk style, with drop d tuning, running scale passages and mixolydian mode harmonies, inspired by the work of the late John Renbourn.

Watch James perform the advanced version by pointing your mobile phone or tablet with a QR code reader at the box on the right.

Or go to the following URL:

https://www.youtube.com/watch?v=MjcxHV9hEbg

The Holly and the Ivy: Beginners

The Holly and the Ivy: Intermediate

The Holly and the Ivy: Advanced

75

While Shepherds Watched Their Flocks

While Shepherds Watched their Flocks is set to a traditional English folk tune called Winchester Old. The text was by the 17th century poet laureate Nahum Tate.

The advanced arrangement of While Shepherds Watched features the melody played in a tremolo style over an arpeggiated accompaniment after the famous Recuerdos de la Alhambra of Francesco Tarrega.

Watch James perform the advanced version by pointing your mobile phone or tablet with a QR code reader at the box on the right.

Or go to the following URL:

https://www.youtube.com/watch?v=Xy3zFNlpPtk

While Shepherds Watched Their Flocks: Beginners

While Shepherds Watched Their Flocks: Intermediate

While Shepherds Watched Their Flocks: Advanced

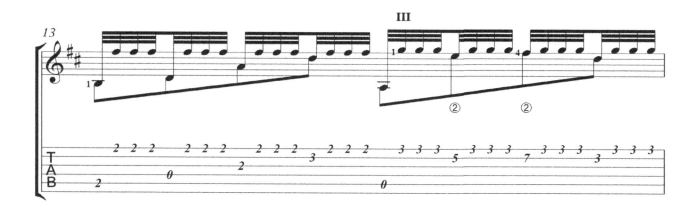

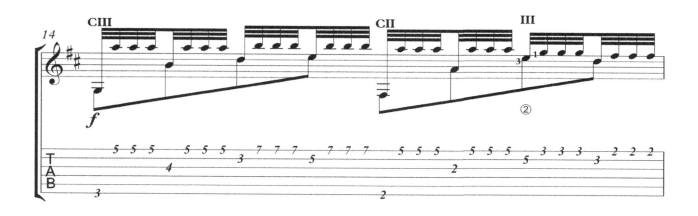

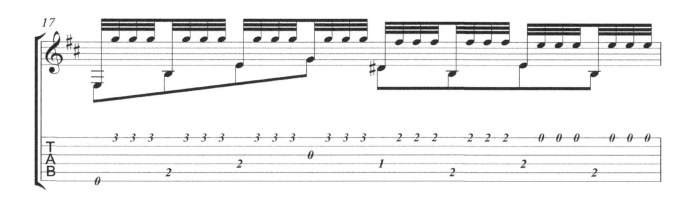
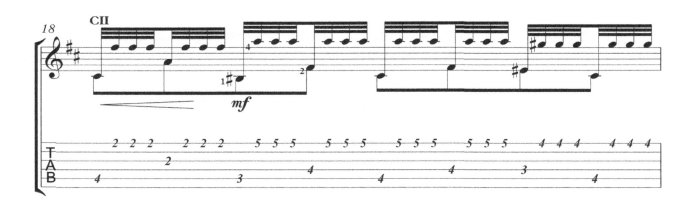
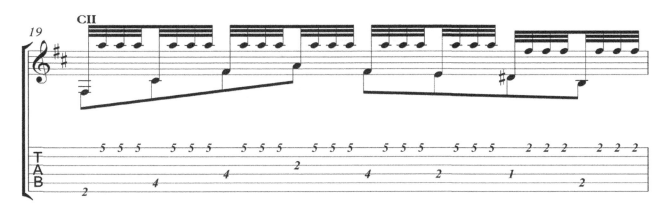

Happy Birthday

Happy Birthday is not, of course, a Christmas carol but it is a useful tune to know, all year round and worthy of inclusion in a book of songs of celebration.

The advanced Happy Birthday is a mini virtuoso showcase in the style of the great 19th century instrumental composers, Paganini, Liszt and Tarrega. It accompanies the familiar tune with a range of arpeggios utilising the full range of the guitar and some florid ornamentation.

Watch James perform the advanced version by pointing your mobile phone or tablet with a QR code reader at the box on the right.

Or go to the following URL:

https://www.youtube.com/watch?v=WOXRqBeb0og

Happy Birthday: Beginners

Happy Birthday: Intermediate

Happy Birthday: Advanced

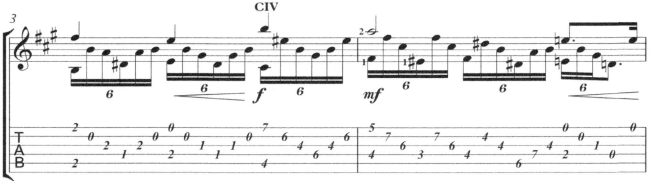

Enjoyed this book? Check out the first book in the series!

Graded arrangements of 12 favorite Christmas songs for acoustic, fingerstyle and classical guitar players.

A collection of twelve of arguably the most well known Christmas carols and holiday season songs beautifully arranged for guitar by guitarist James Akers.

Each of the 12 songs are offered at beginner, intermediate and advanced technical versions. For beginners, start with the easy version of the song, then build up to the more complex versions which are all found in one book. This publication would also be an excellent resource for guitar teachers looking for potential material for students around Christmas time.

All songs are notated in both music and guitar TAB for non music readers.

All advanced versions of the song come with QR codes for watching a video performance of each song.

THE TWELVE SONGS INCLUDED ARE:

- Auld Lang Syne

- Away in a Manger

- Ding Dong Merrily on High

- God Rest Ye Merry Gentlemen

- Good King Wenceslas

- In Dulci Jubilo

- Jingle Bells

- O Christmas Tree

- Silent Night

- The Twelve Days of Christmas

- We Three Kings of Orient Are

- We Wish You a Merry Christmas

CHRISTMAS CAROLS FOR GUITAR

Graded arrangements of 12 favourite Christmas songs for acoustic, fingerstyle and classical guitar

Arranged by James Akers

Each song offered at three ability levels: Beginner - Intermediate - Advanced

Songs include: Auld Lang Syne, Away in a manger, God Rest Ye Merry Gentlemen, Jingle Bells, O Christmas Tree, Silent Night

GM

FREE DOWNLOAD OF EXTRA MATERIAL

A link is included within the book to download free extra material which accompanies the publication. Contents of download:

- mp3 versions of all advanced versions of the Christmas carol guitar arrangements for you to listen to before practice.

- mp3 accompanying tracks for the beginner versions of the Christmas carols for play along.

- A PDF book which details all the chords used in the beginner guitar chord arrangements offered in chord diagram format for easy understanding.

About James Akers

Critically acclaimed musician Jamie Akers was hailed as 'the great Scottish guitarist' by Classical Guitar Magazine and, in a review from Gramophone, his playing was described as, 'containing all the warmth, colour and expressive richness one could hope for.' Jamie has, throughout a varied career, explored various genres of music from a historical and stylistic perspective, combining diligent research with expressive performances to communicate the continuity of musical endeavour through the centuries.

Jamie was born in Scotland and began playing guitar at the age of 10. Initially playing rock and blues then attempting to play jazz and finally settling on the classical guitar, he was largely self-taught before having lessons with Robert Mackillop at Napier University, Edinburgh. Whilst at Napier he turned his attentions to playing the lute and pursued this as his principle study at the Royal College of Music, with Jakob Lindberg. Having added the Theorbo to his expanding instrument collection, Jamie completed his studies at Trinity College of Music, studying with Jacob Heringman and David Miller, with additional lessons and advice from Paul O'Dette and Elizabeth Kenny. Settled on the period instrument path, Jamie continued accumulating instruments and exploring the music of the 16th to 19th centuries, with occasional forays into contemporary music.

Following a Junior Fellowship at Trinity College of Music Jamie began pursuing a varied professional career. As a soloist he has performed throughout Europe, the Middle East and Australia, giving recitals at the Edinburgh Fringe Festival, Ullapool Guitar Festival, Classical Guitar Retreat, Exeter Guitar Festival, the Yorke Music Trust, the Italian Cultural Institute, in the L'Oratoire de Lourve, and the Copenhagen Renaissance Music Festival.

He has accompanied leading singers including Dame Emma Kirkby, James Laing, Miriam Allan, Claire Wilkinson and Jake Arditti and is the staff accompanist for the John Kerr memorial song prize. Jamie has performed with many early music ensembles such as I Fagiolini, Ex Cathedra, Stile Antico, the Marian Consort, Fretwork, Chelys Viol Consort, The Rose Consort of Viols, The Parley of Instruments, The Hanover Band, The Brook Street Band, Sounds Baroque and the Dunedin Consort.

As a continuo player Jamie has worked for major opera companies, English National Opera, Welsh National Opera, Opera North, Longborough festival opera and Innsbruck Festival Opera and orchestras and chamber groups including The Scottish, Irish and English Chamber Orchestras, Northern Sinfonia, the Royal Scottish National Orchestra, The Ulster Orchestra, The Essen Philharmonie, The Scottish Ensemble, with trumpeter Alison Balsom, and ventured into indie folk-rock with Damon Albarn.

Jamie has performed on numerous recordings; a few film soundtracks; several theatrical stages, including Shakespeare's Globe Theatre and the Barbican, and broadcast for the BBC, France Musique and RTE Lyric, Ireland, and has been an artist in residence with the renowned Scottish Ensemble.

Jamie lectures in early plucked strings at the Royal Conservatoire of Scotland and teaches annually on the Renaissance Music Week course in Ejstrupholm, Denmark. He has also taught or given masterclasses at, The Royal College of Music, The Royal Northern College of Music, The Royal Welsh College of Music and Drama, the Western Australian Academy of Performing Arts and The Rostov Conservatoire, Russia.

http://jamieakers.com/

More From James Akers From GMI - Guitar & Music Institute

If you have enjoyed this book then we're sure you will also find James's transcriptions of Theorbo music for classical guitar a must buy.

Not only does the book include beautiful works by Kapsberger, Piccinini and Castaldi but this large publication also includes the following:

All works offered in both music and guitar tabulature.

Selected works include an audio commentary that is accessed via QR codes placed alongside specific titles. Use your mobile (cell) phone or tablet to listen to James's commentary from both a technical and musical perspective about the work you will be learning.

Selected works include a QR code that opens up a performance video of the piece currently being considered. Listen to this stellar guitarist play and interpret the musical composition for your guidance as well as listening pleasure.

Owners of the book will be able to access further musical works that accompany this publication. Your copy of this book will include a code which enables you to access this PDF download completely free of charge.

Italian Theorbo Music is available to purchase from Amazon and all other good online sellers in both printed and electronic format. A wire bound flat lie version of the book is available only from https://gmiguitarshop.com

An introduction PDF book containing extra works for pre sale of this book or as mentioned free for those who have already purchased the printed version is available to buy direct from the GMI - Guitar & Music Institute online shop at https://gmiguitarshop.com

RECORDING

James Akers' critically acclaimed recording of Scottish Romantic Guitar Music, The Soldier's Return, is available on CD and through various digital platforms.

Visit www.resonusclassics.com for more information.

Another Great Title By James Akers From GMI - Guitar & Music Institute

If you have enjoyed this book then we're sure you will also find James's transcriptions found in Scottish Classical Guitar Collection Volume 1 an absolute must have.

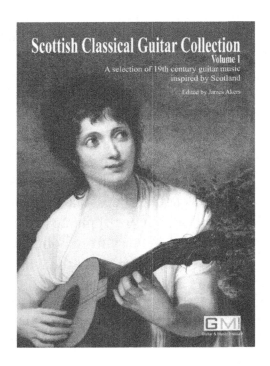

For the intermediate to advanced player, this volume of work includes Mauro Giuliani's beautiful settings of six favourite Scottish songs; Fernando Sor's masterful 'Variations on Ye Banks and Braes' and Johan Kaspar Mertz's dramatic evocation of the landscape of the Outer Hebrides, 'Fingal's Cave.'

Scottish Classical Guitar Collection Volume 1 is available to purchase from Amazon and all other good online sellers in both printed and electronic format. PDF versions of individual songs found within the book are available to buy direct from the GMI - Guitar & Music Institute online shop at https://gmiguitarshop.com

There is also a wire bound lie flat version of this publication only available at the GMI Guitar Shop at the web address above.

If you enjoyed this publication, then please visit the following websites for more content, lessons, articles, videos, podcasts, free and paid content and more…

We'd also really appreciate a positive review on Amazon if you found this book enjoyable and an addition to your guitar playing experience.

www.guitarandmusicinstitute.com

gmiguitarshop.com

USING THE QR CODES…WHAT'S A QR CODE READER?

If you are not familiar with a QR code, it's the box shown on every title page of a song and has strange marks on it.

Using a search engine of your choice, type in "free QR code reader", there are many to choose from. Select one and download it to your cell/mobile phone or tablet.

Once installed, open the app up and point it at one of the squares, keeping your hand steady. It will recognise the web address in the box and notify you once it has worked it's magic.

It will offer to open up the video that has been added to the QR box you are pointing at. You can watch and listen to the song or use the opened video to play along with the song.

Made in the USA
Monee, IL
31 March 2023

30999865R00052